MW00436114

? Essential Question
What do myths help us understand?

The **APPLES** *of* **IDUN**

adapted by Betsy Hebert

illustrated by Valeria Cis

Chapter 1

THE EAGLE

Long ago, the gods liked to walk on Earth. Loki and Odin had been hiking for many days. The two gods were very hungry.

Odin killed an ox, and Loki made a fire. But the pieces of meat would not cook.

Was this someone's trick? Loki, who had played plenty of tricks himself, looked around. No one appeared.

Then a voice spoke from above. "I will make the meat cook if you will share it." Loki and Odin looked up. A huge eagle sat on a high tree branch and rustled his wings.

"Yes, you may have some meat," Odin said.

So the meat cooked, and the eagle swooped down. He grabbed many large pieces of meat. Loki, who was very hungry, jumped up. He was angry. He grabbed a big piece of wood and hit the eagle.

Poor Loki! The wood stuck to the eagle's claws. The other end stuck to Loki's hands. This was not a real eagle. It was a storm giant in the form of an eagle.

STOP AND CHECK

Who is Loki? What has happened so far?

6

Chapter 2

THE APPLES

The eagle flew off, dragging Loki with him. Loki banged and bumped into trees and rocks. "Please," he begged. "Let me go!"

"I will let you go if you do one thing for me," the eagle said. "I want the apples of Idun."

Loki said, "Oh, no, I can't do that!"

The apples of Idun were special. The goddess Idun grew beautiful golden apples. She fed them to the gods. The apples kept the gods young.

Loki did not want to steal them. But he was soon tired of being dragged. "Yes," he said. "I'll get the apples."

So the giant eagle dropped Loki.

8

Loki limped home and then went to Idun. The goddess was putting her apples into a basket.

"Those are beautiful apples," Loki said, smiling at her.

"Yes," Idun replied. "There are no others like them."

"Really?" said Loki. "I saw a tree filled with apples that looked just like those. It is growing at the edge of the city."

"Show me this tree," Idun said.

"I will," said Loki. "Bring your apples with you. Then you can compare them to the others."

STOP AND CHECK

What is special about Idun's apples?

Chapter 3

THE CHASE

Idun took her basket of apples and followed Loki.

But as soon as Idun left the city, the storm giant snatched her. He grabbed the goddess in his eagle claws. In moments, they were gone.

The next morning, the gods waited
for Idun to bring their apples. She
did not come. The gods searched for
Idun. They looked and looked. Days
went by. The gods began to grow
old. Their skin wrinkled, and their
shining hair turned dull and gray.

Then the gods found out that Loki
had tricked Idun. They were angry.
"How could you do that?" they said.

"I'm sorry! I will get her back," Loki
said. He turned into a falcon and
flew to the storm giant's home.

Loki found Idun at the giant's house.
He turned the goddess and her
apples into nuts. Then he put them
in Idun's basket. He held the basket
and flew off as fast as he could.

But the storm giant saw Loki and
flew after him.

The gods saw this, rushed to the city walls, and made piles of wood. As soon as Loki flew over the walls, the gods lit the wood on fire.

Huge flames leaped up, and the eagle flew into the fire. Loki, Idun, and the apples were safe. Idun fed the gods, and they grew young again. Loki had fixed his mistake.

STOP AND CHECK

How did Loki get the apples back?

Respond to Reading

Summarize

Use important details to summarize what happens in *The Apples of Idun*.

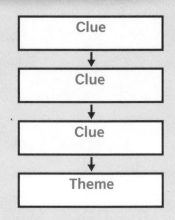

Text Evidence

1. How do you know *The Apples of Idun* is a myth? Genre

2. What is the overall idea this myth tells about? Theme

3. Use sentence clues to figure out the meaning of the word *searched* on page 12. Sentence Clues

4. Write about what the apples did. Give details. Write About Reading

Compare Texts
Read about another golden fruit.

Tomatoes

Tomatoes come
in many colors.

flower

fruit

fruit

stem

The green tomatoes are not ripe yet.

Tomatoes develop in stages. First, a yellow flower grows. Then a green tomato forms. The fruit ripens and turns red or yellow.

Tomatoes first grew in South America. Today they are grown all over the world. The United States produces a large part of the world's tomato crops.

People eat tomatoes raw and cooked.

How to Grow Tomatoes

1. Put a pot of tomato seeds and soil in a sunny window.
2. Give the seeds water. After six weeks, move the plants outside.
3. Put them in a bigger pot or in the ground. You'll have tomatoes in about three months!

Make Connections
Why did the storm giant punish Loki?
Essential Question

How is a yellow tomato like one of Idun's apples? Text to Text

Focus on Genre

Myth A myth is a type of folktale. It might tell a story about gods or goddesses. It might explain something in nature.

What to Look for The characters in *The Apples of Idun* are gods and goddesses. They have special powers. Idun grows golden apples that keep the gods young.

Your Turn

Plan your own myth about a god or goddess. Give your character a name. Tell what special things he or she can do.